Within the pages of this book you will find 24 various dragon designs for your own colouring creativity. Each page contains a different dragon ready for you to colour in. Simply relax, de-stress yourself and use your own imagination with these wonderful designs.

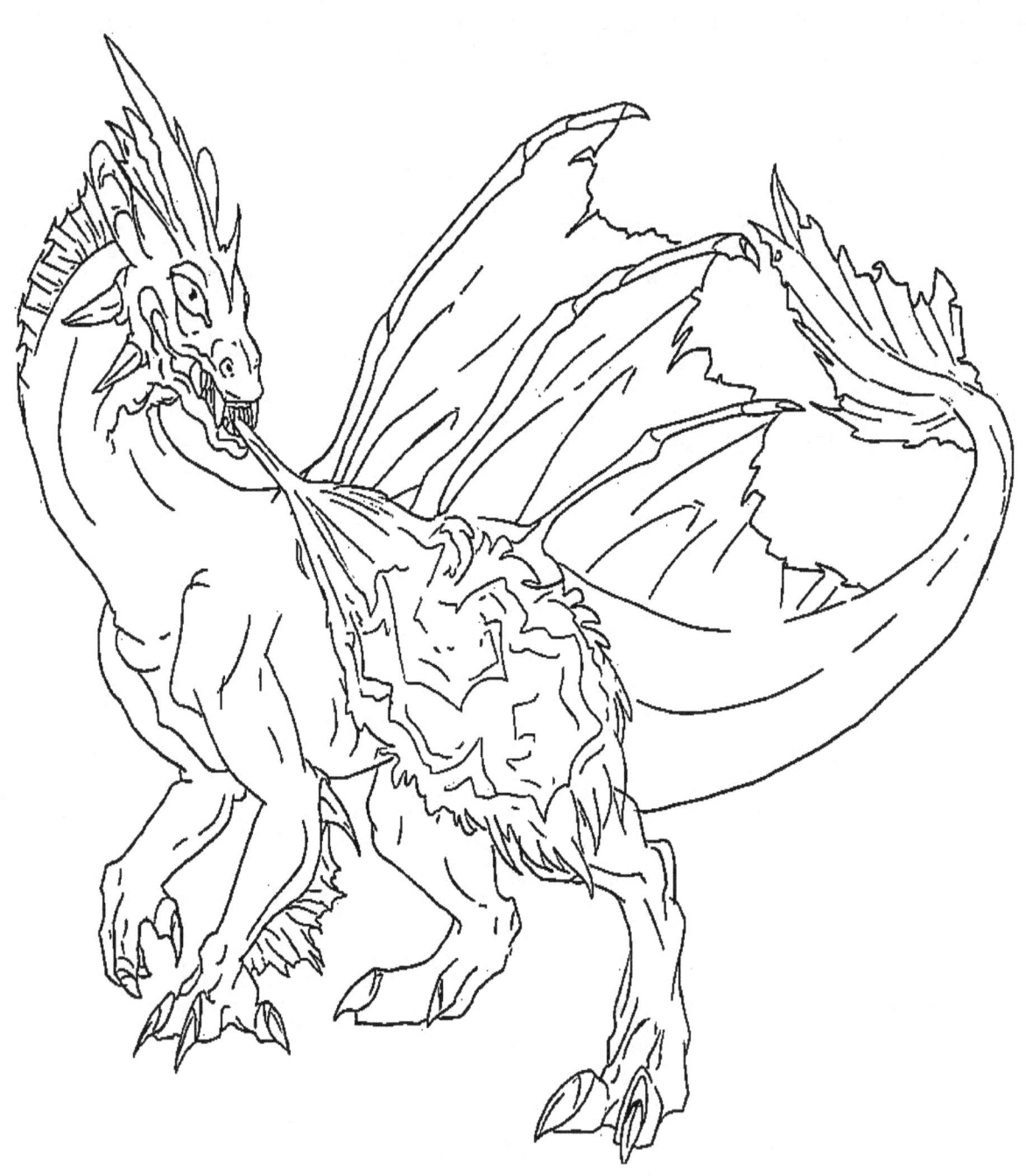

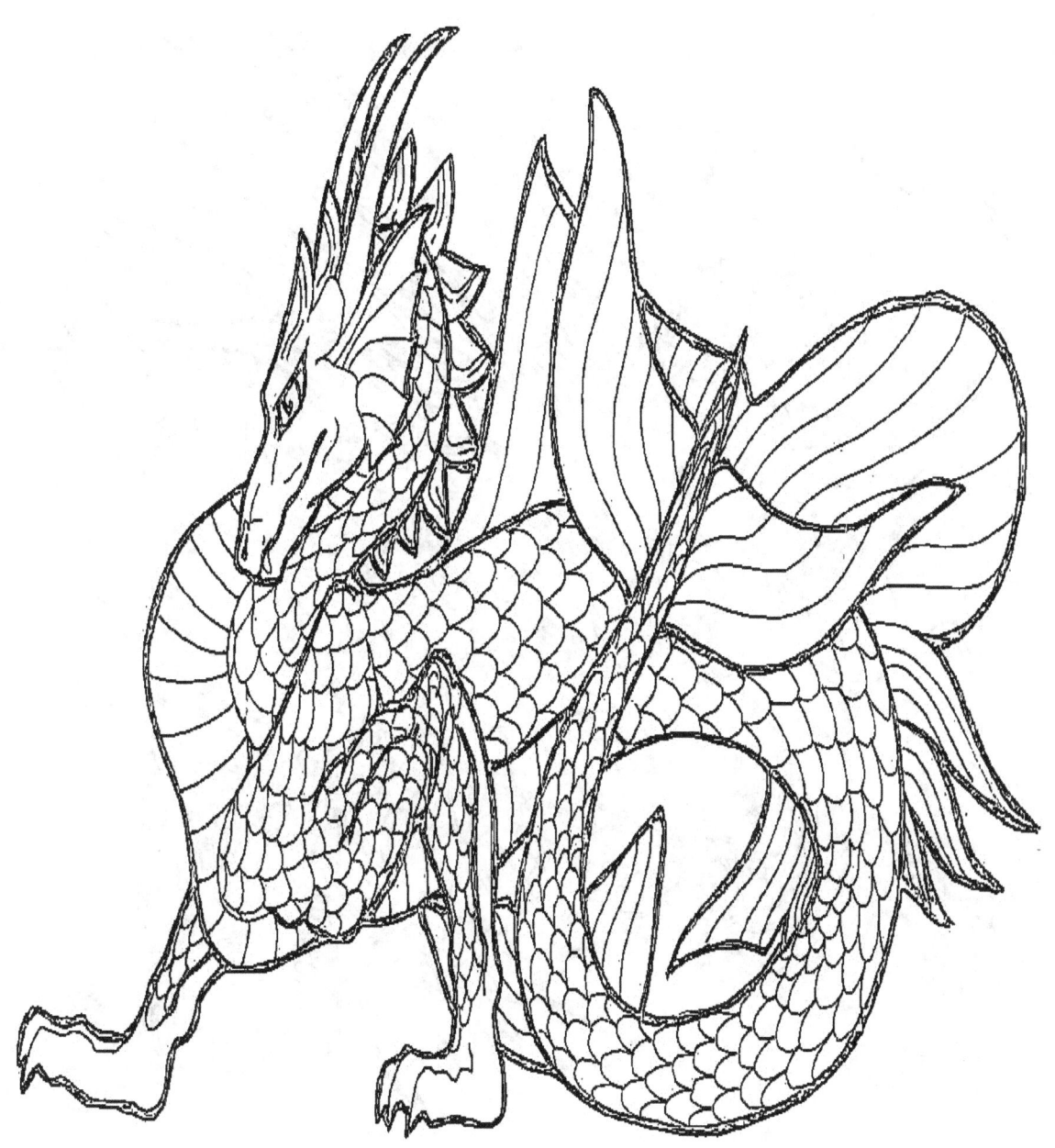

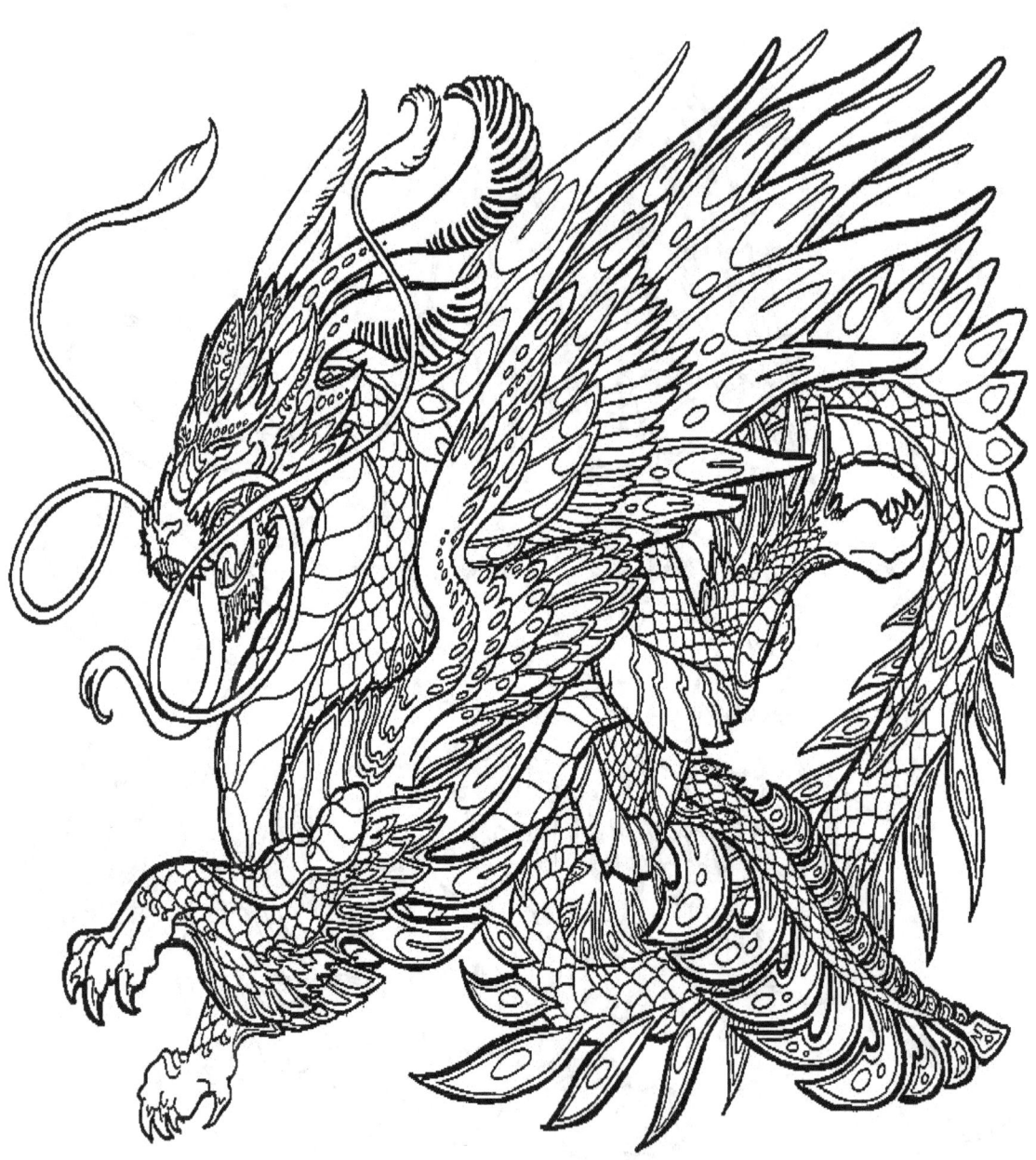

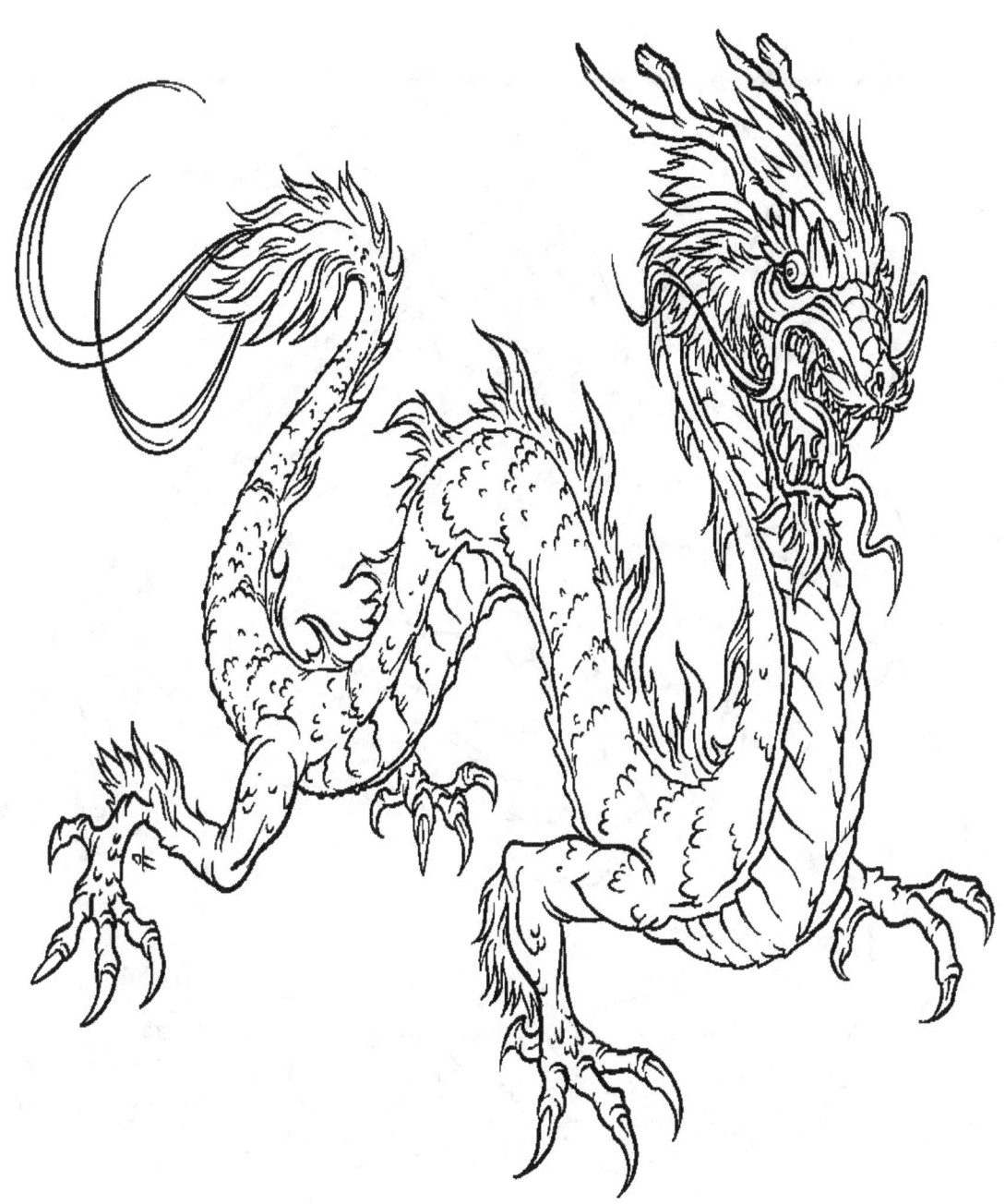

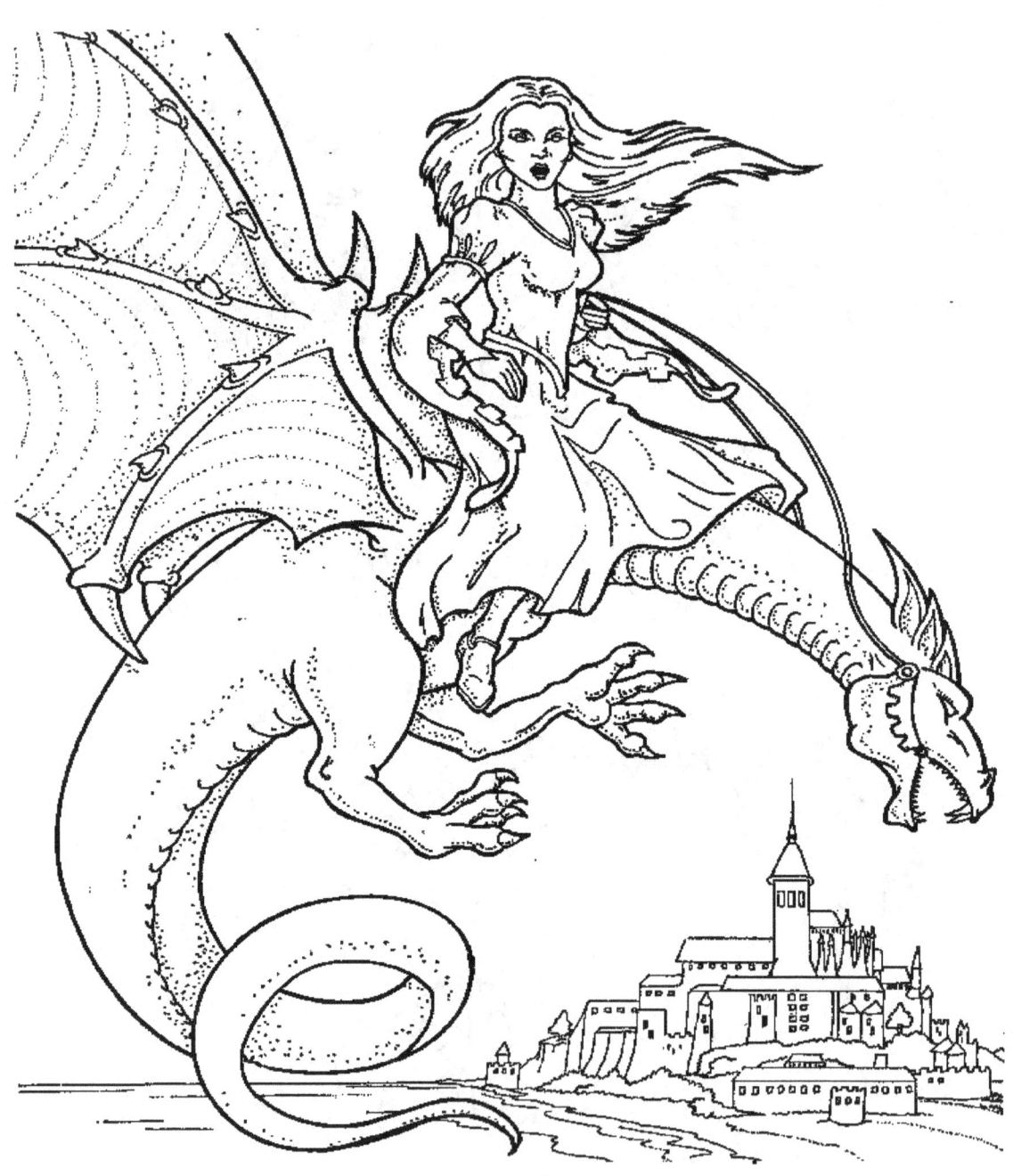

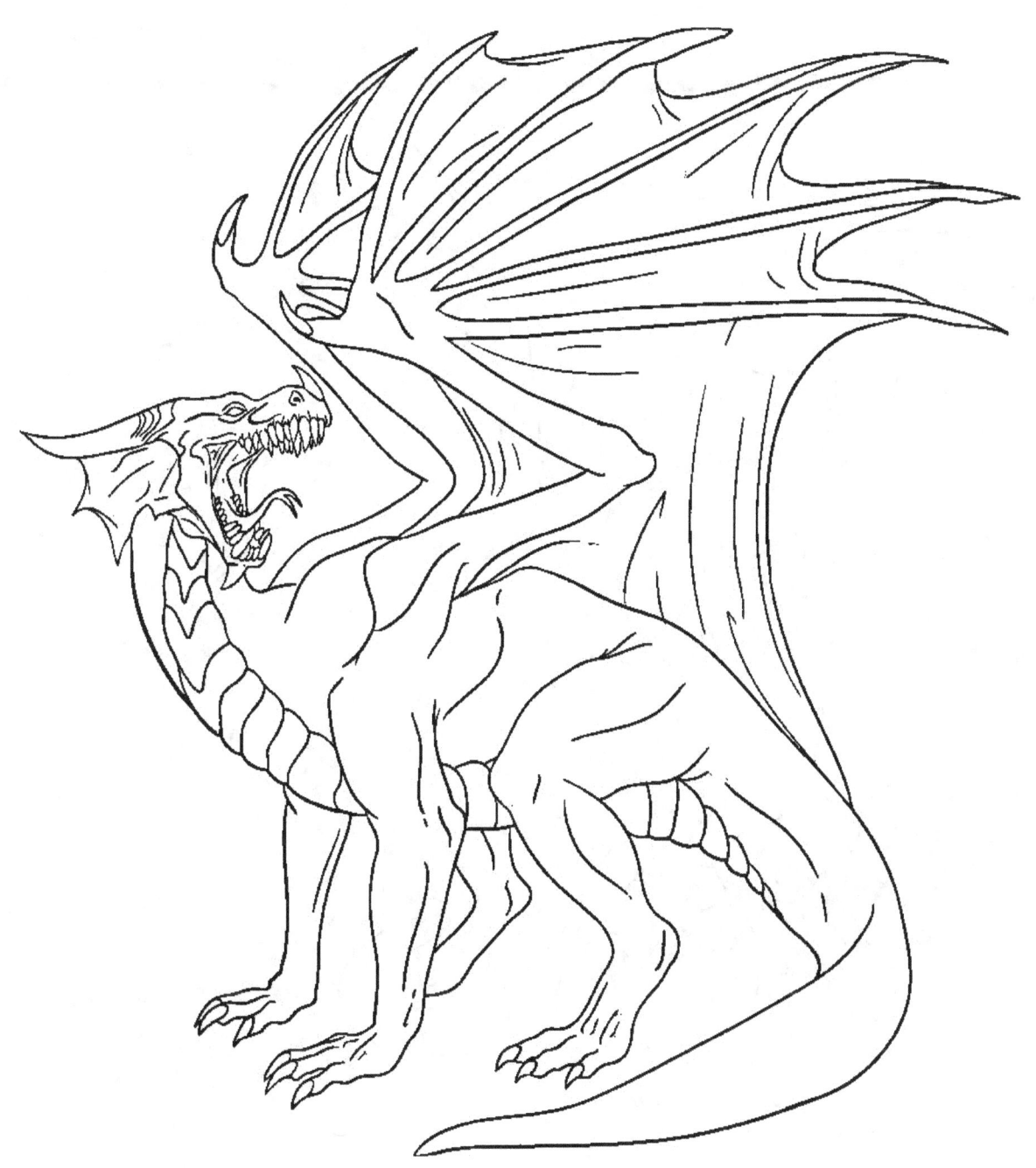

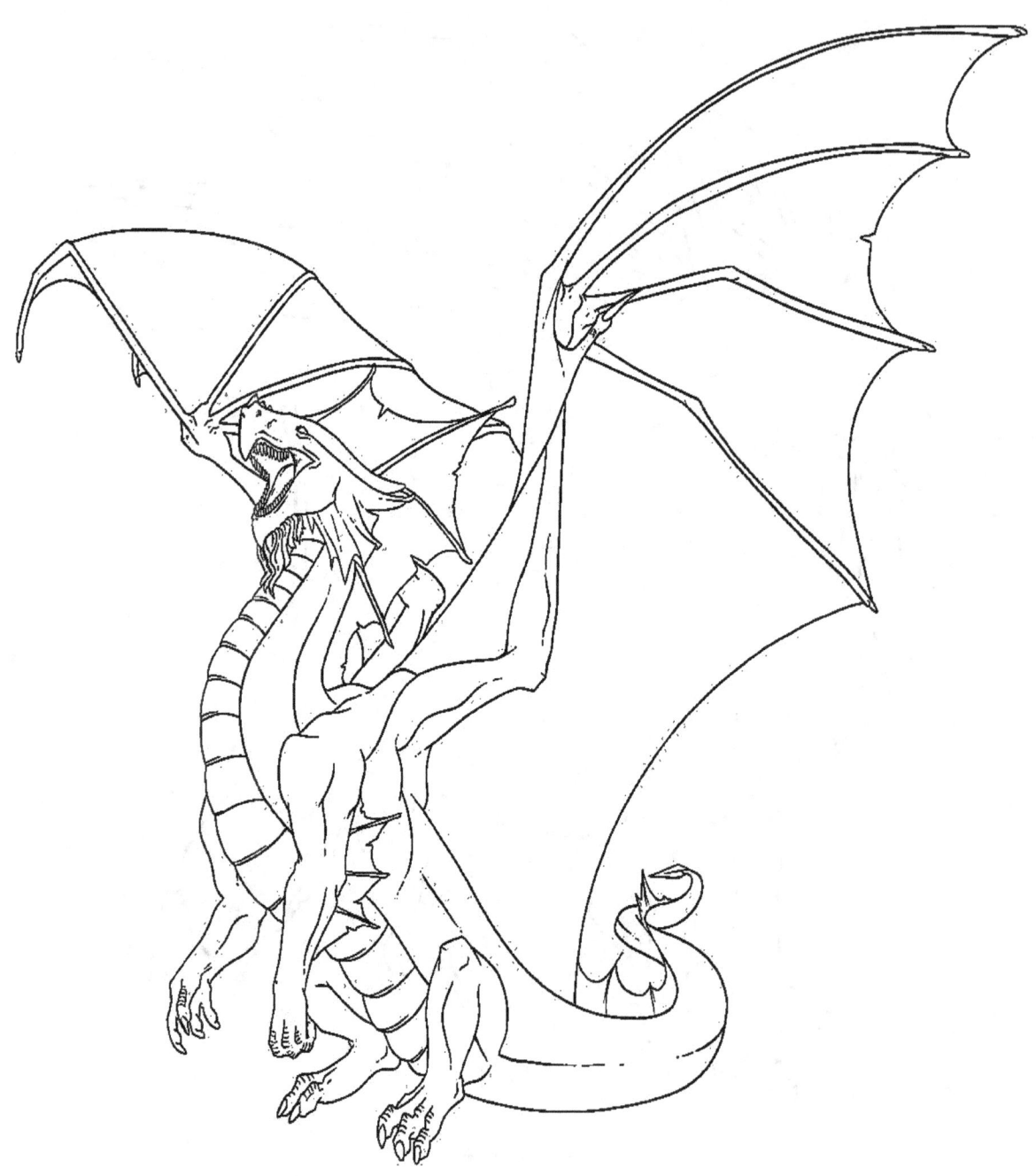

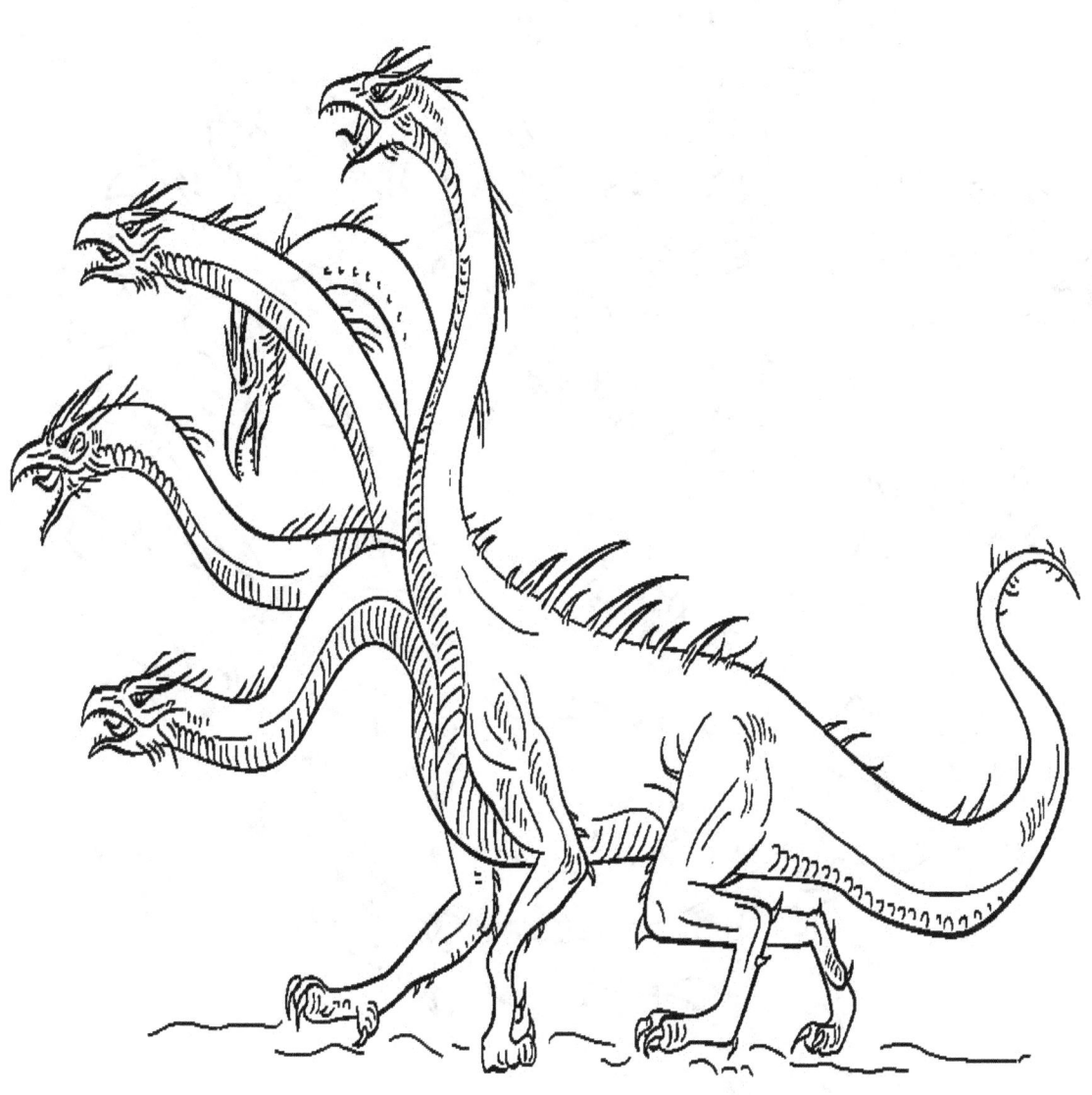

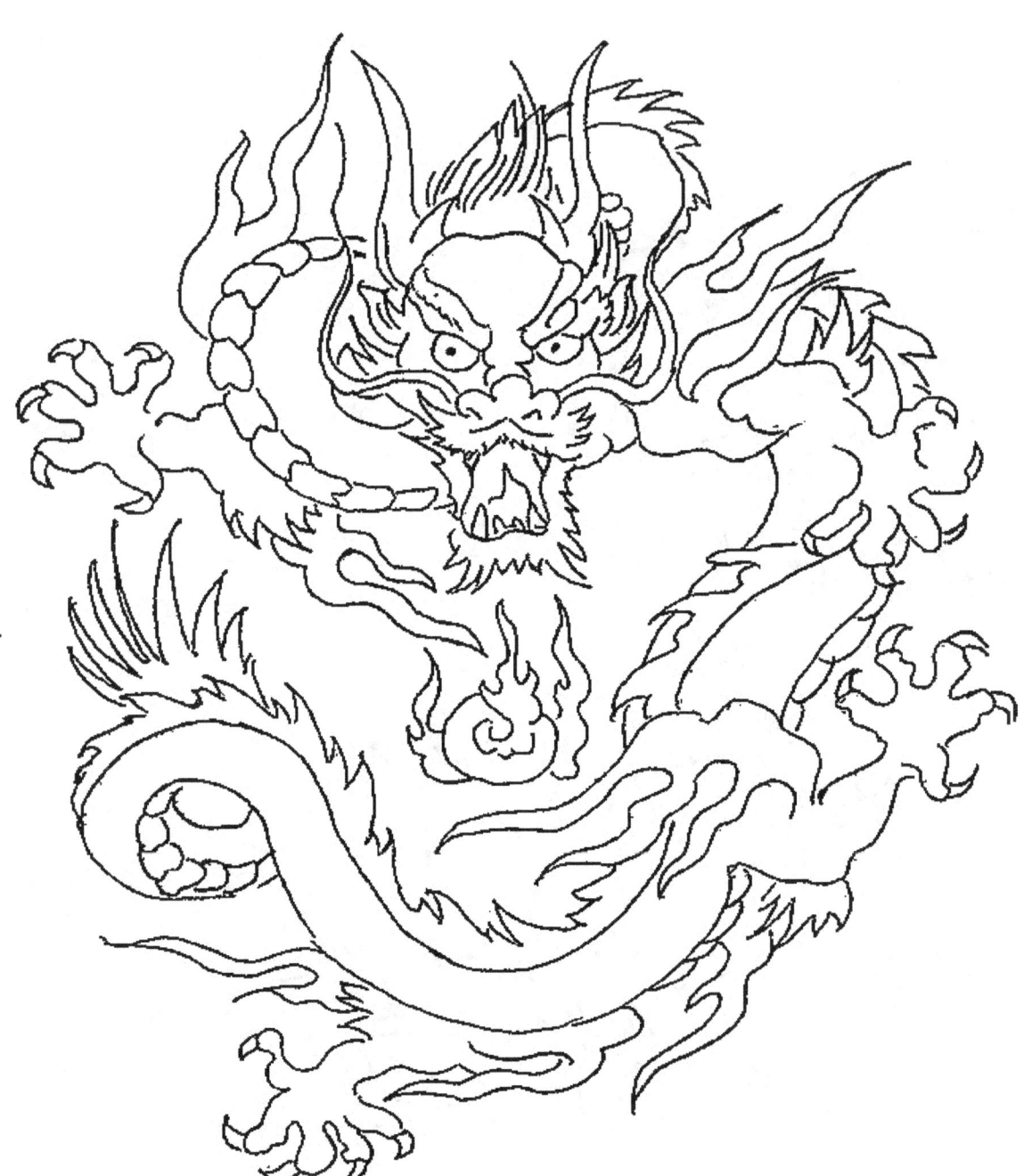

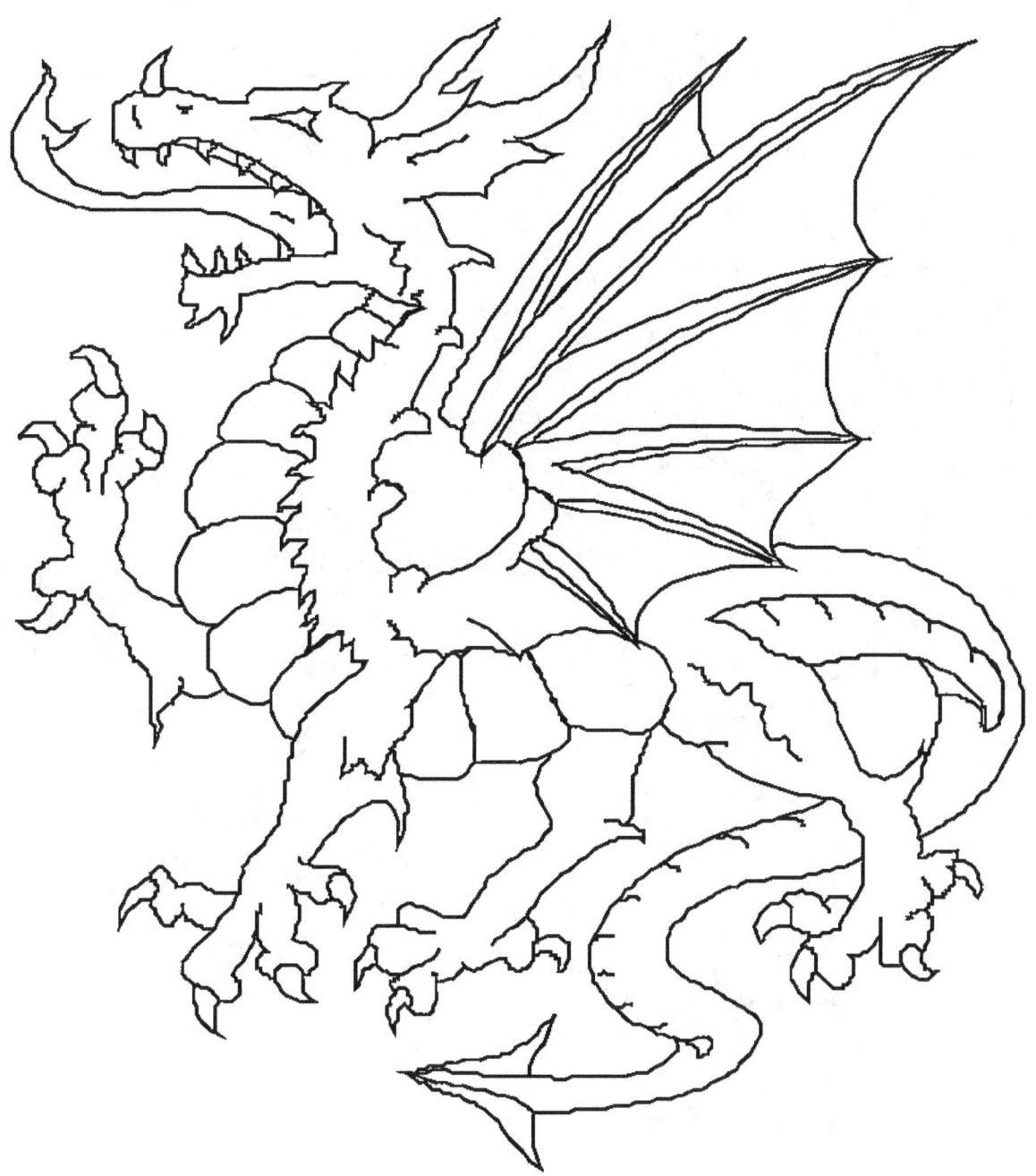

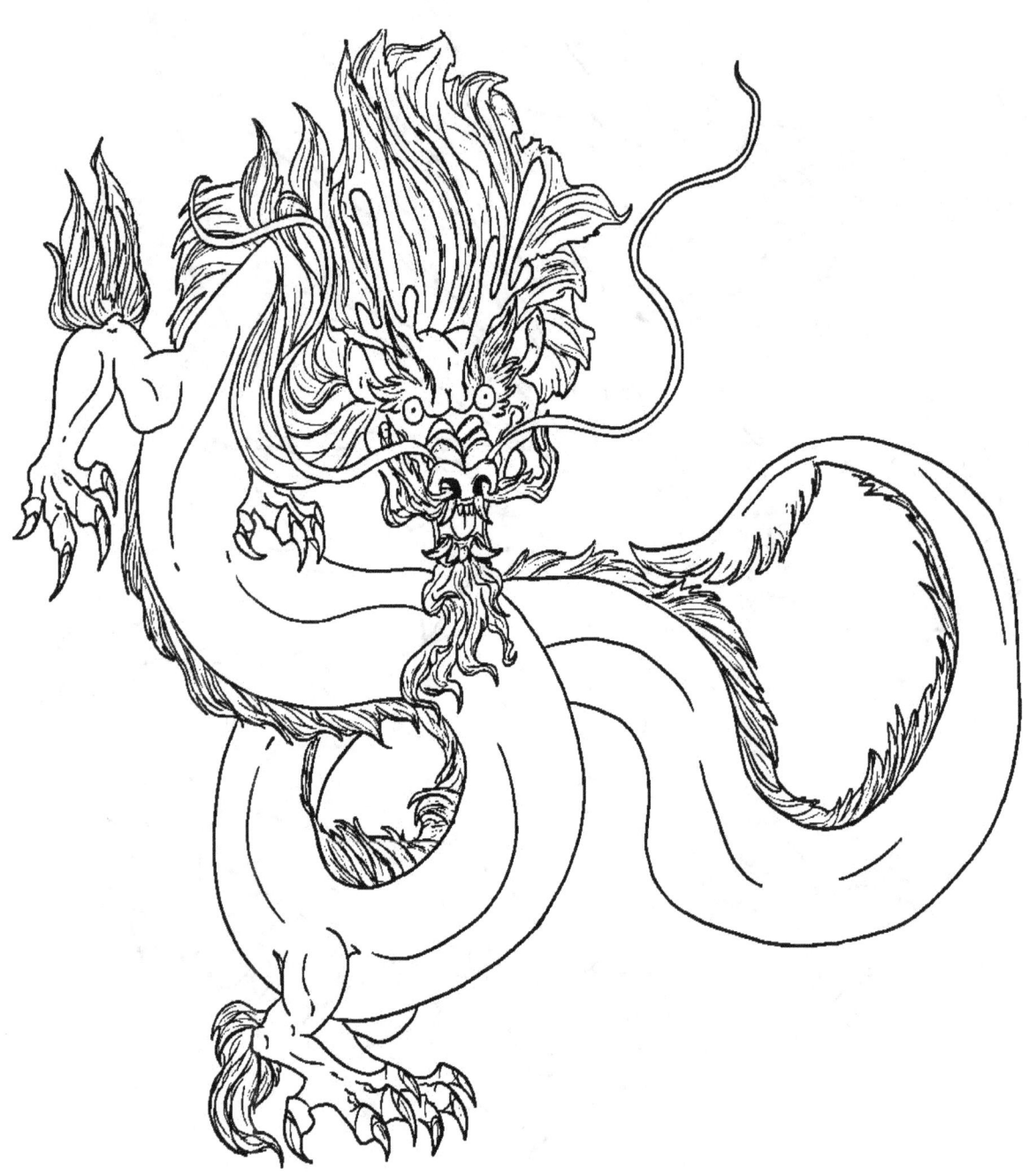

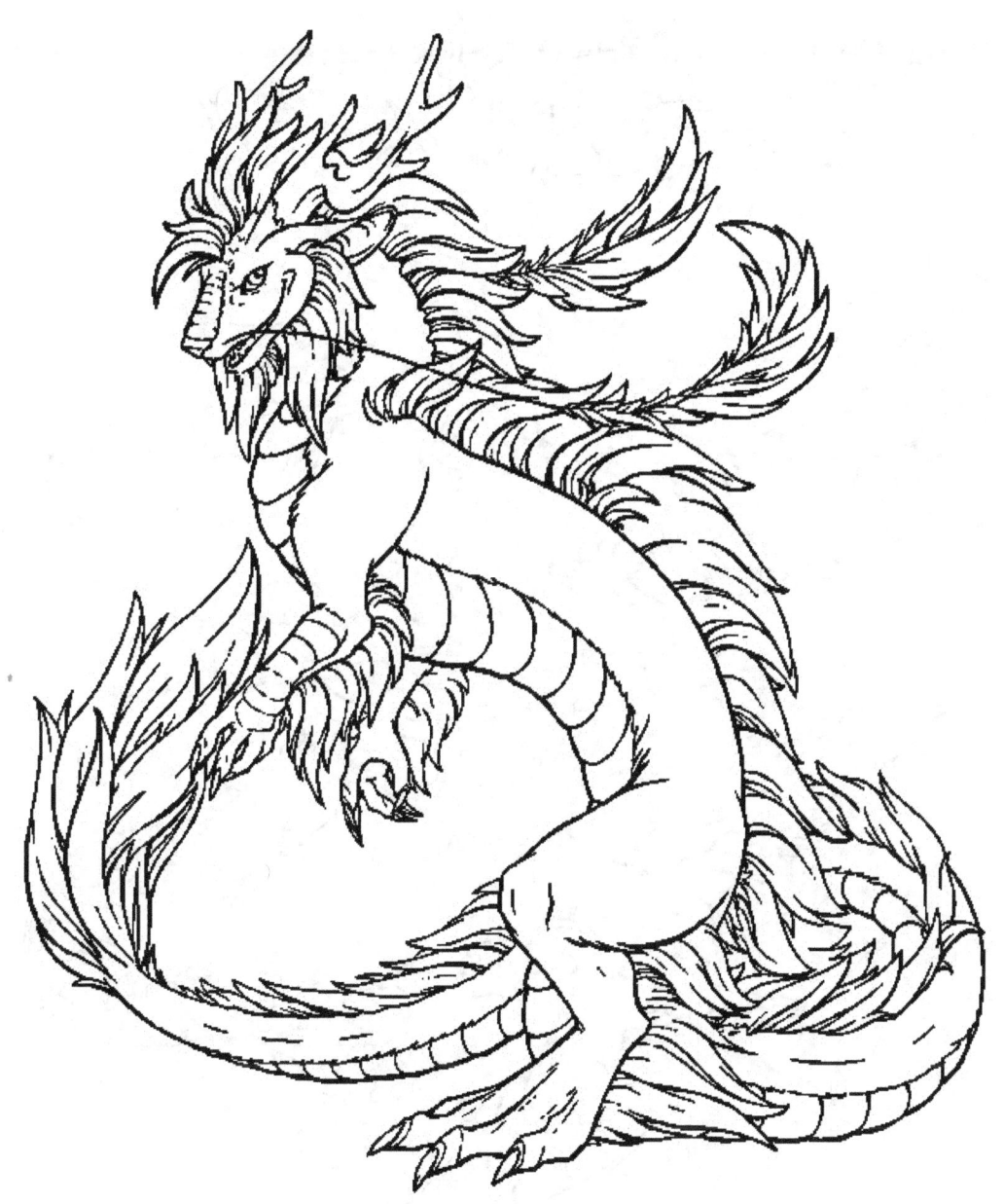

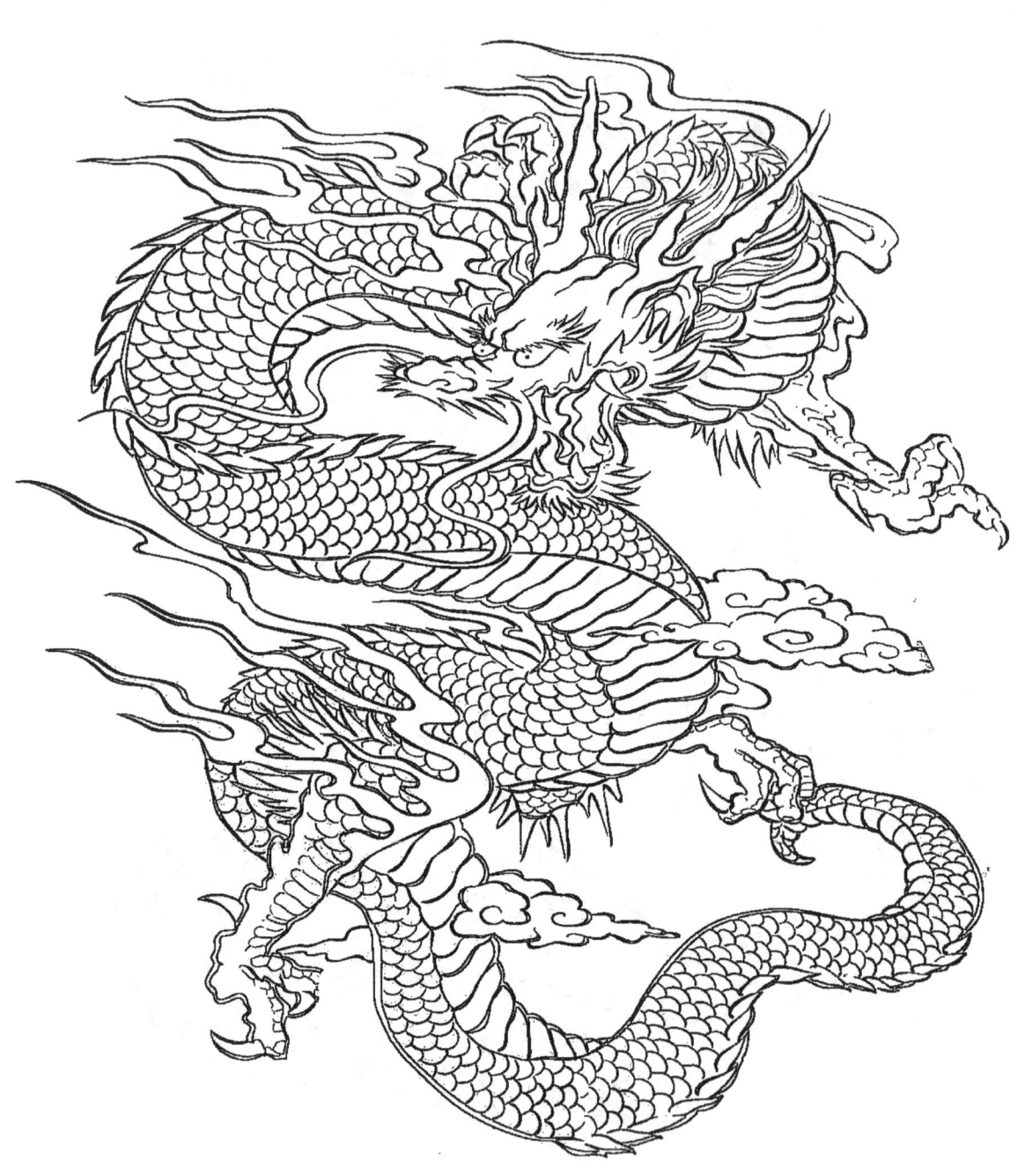

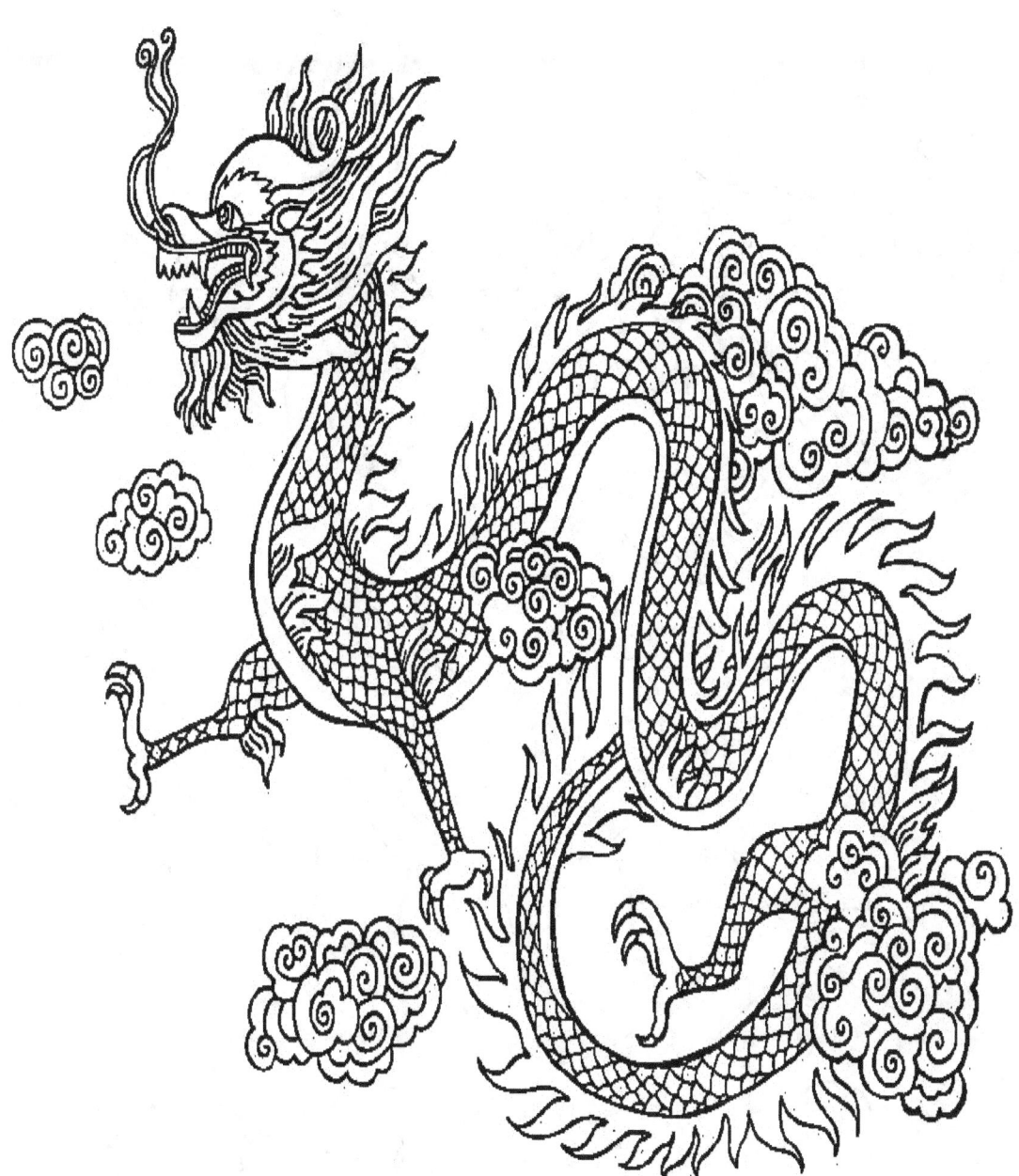

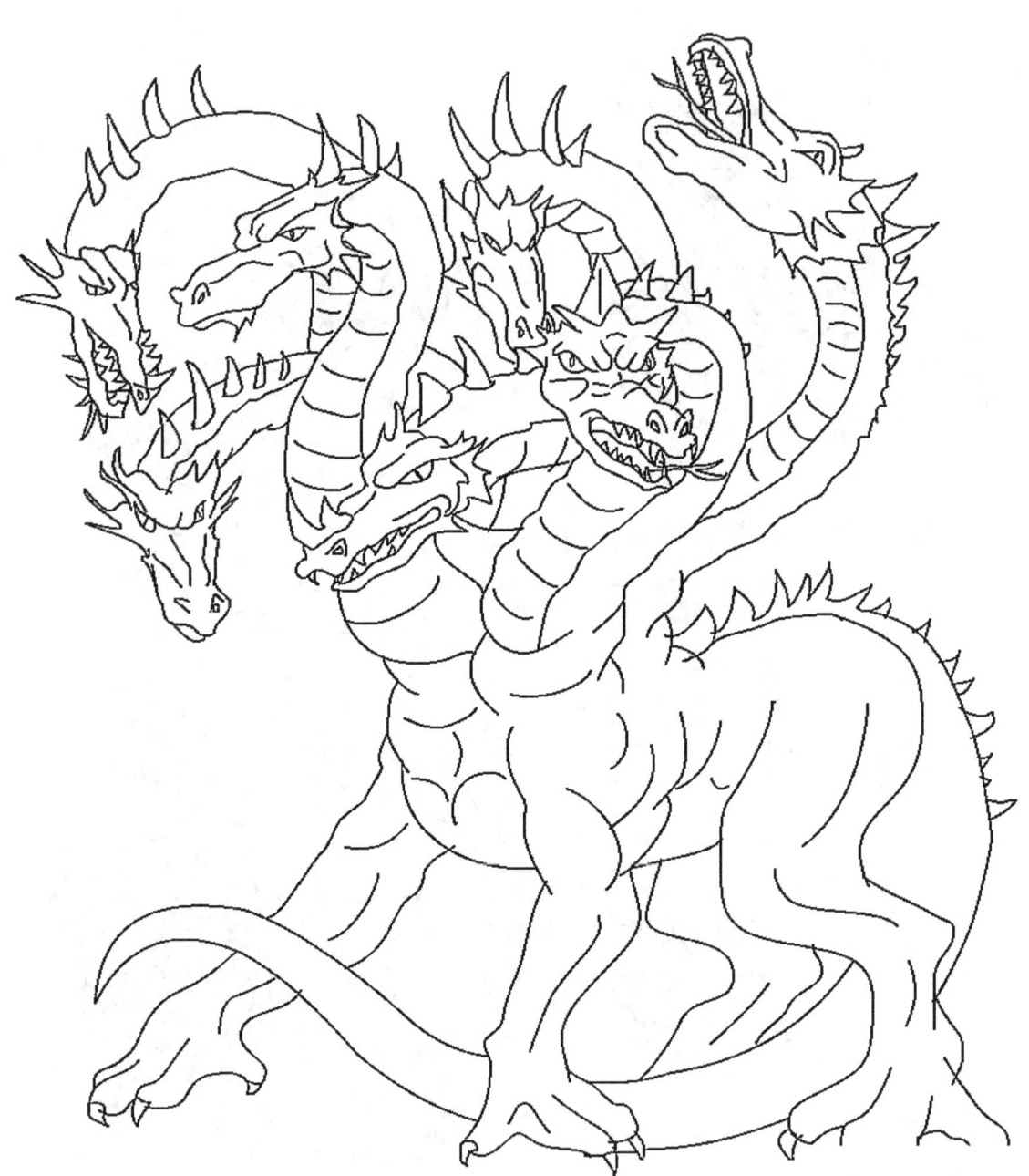

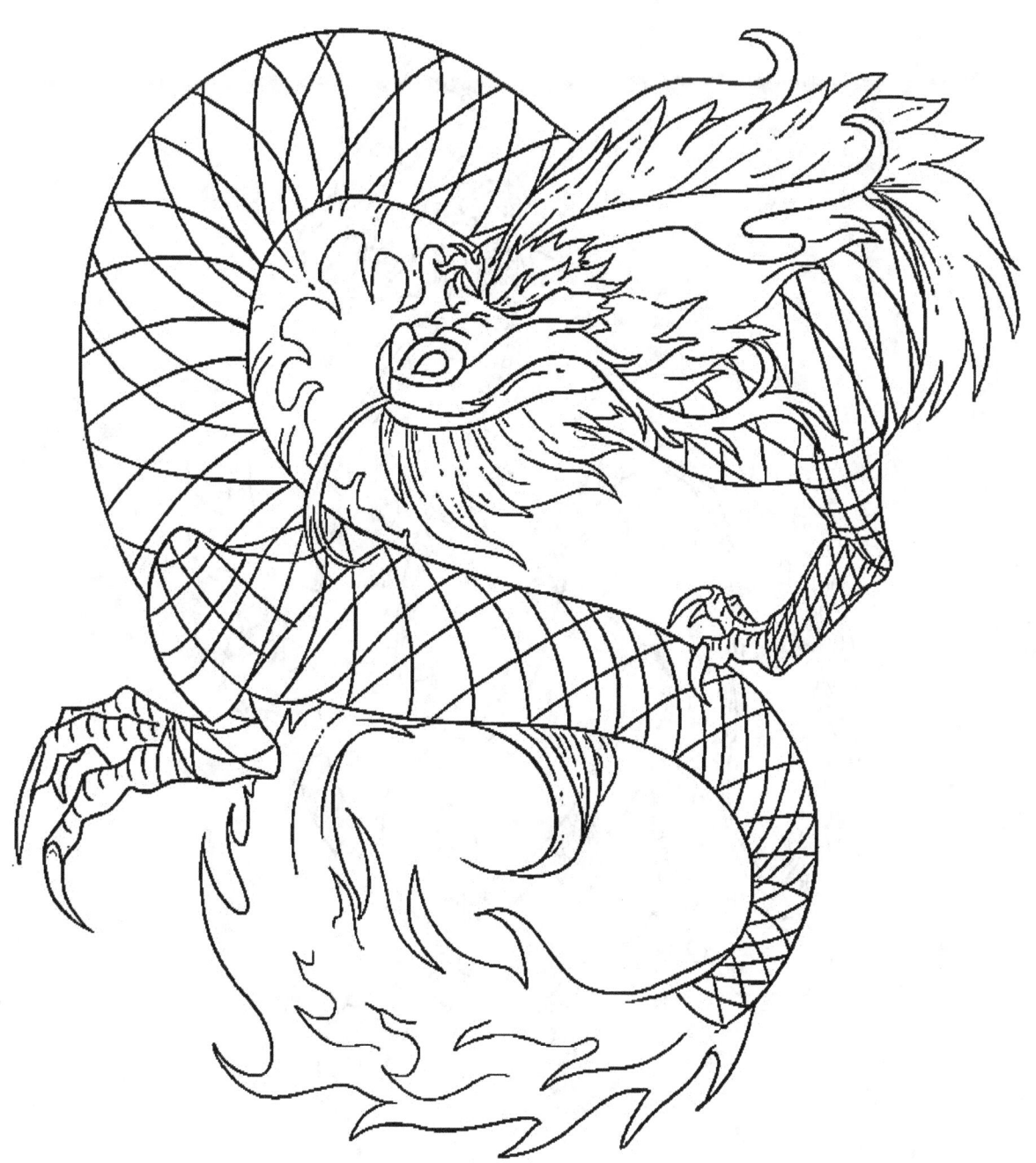

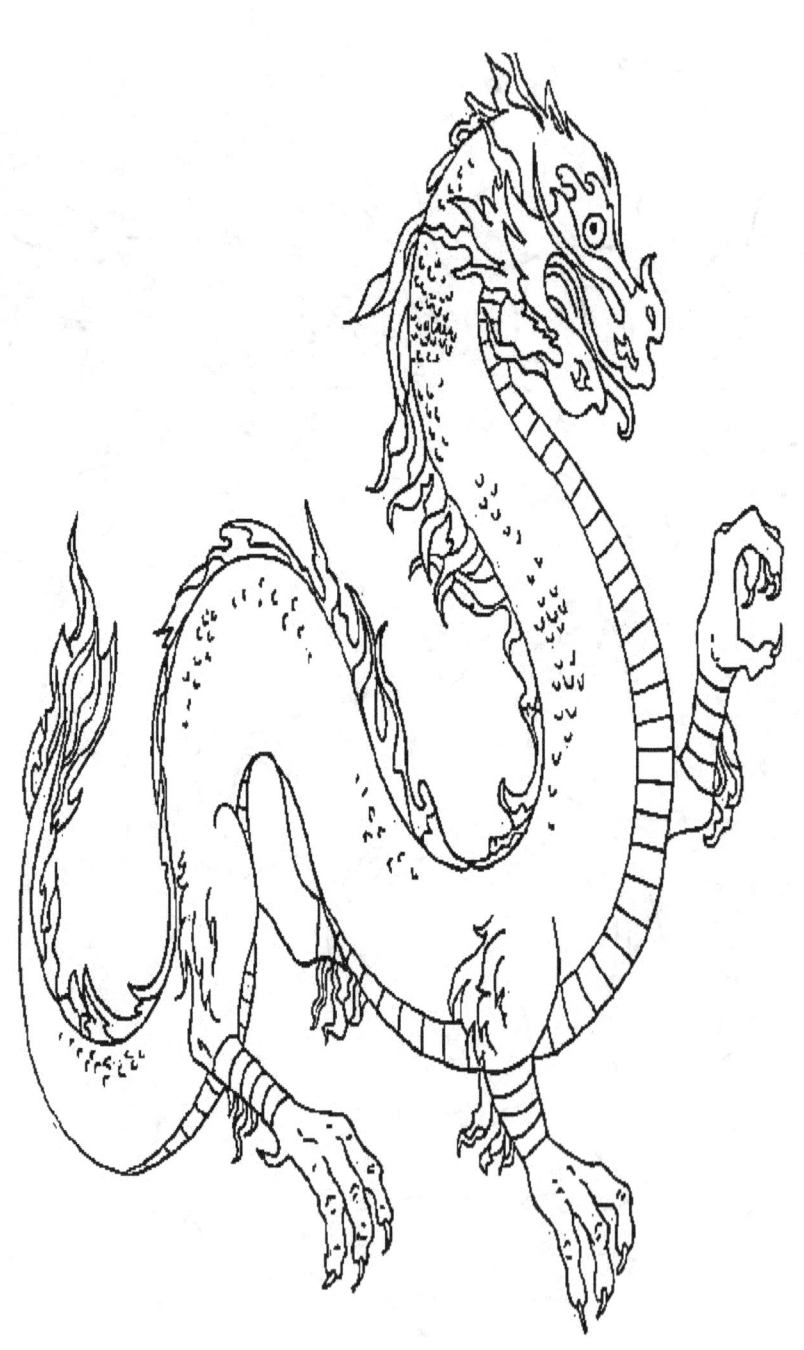

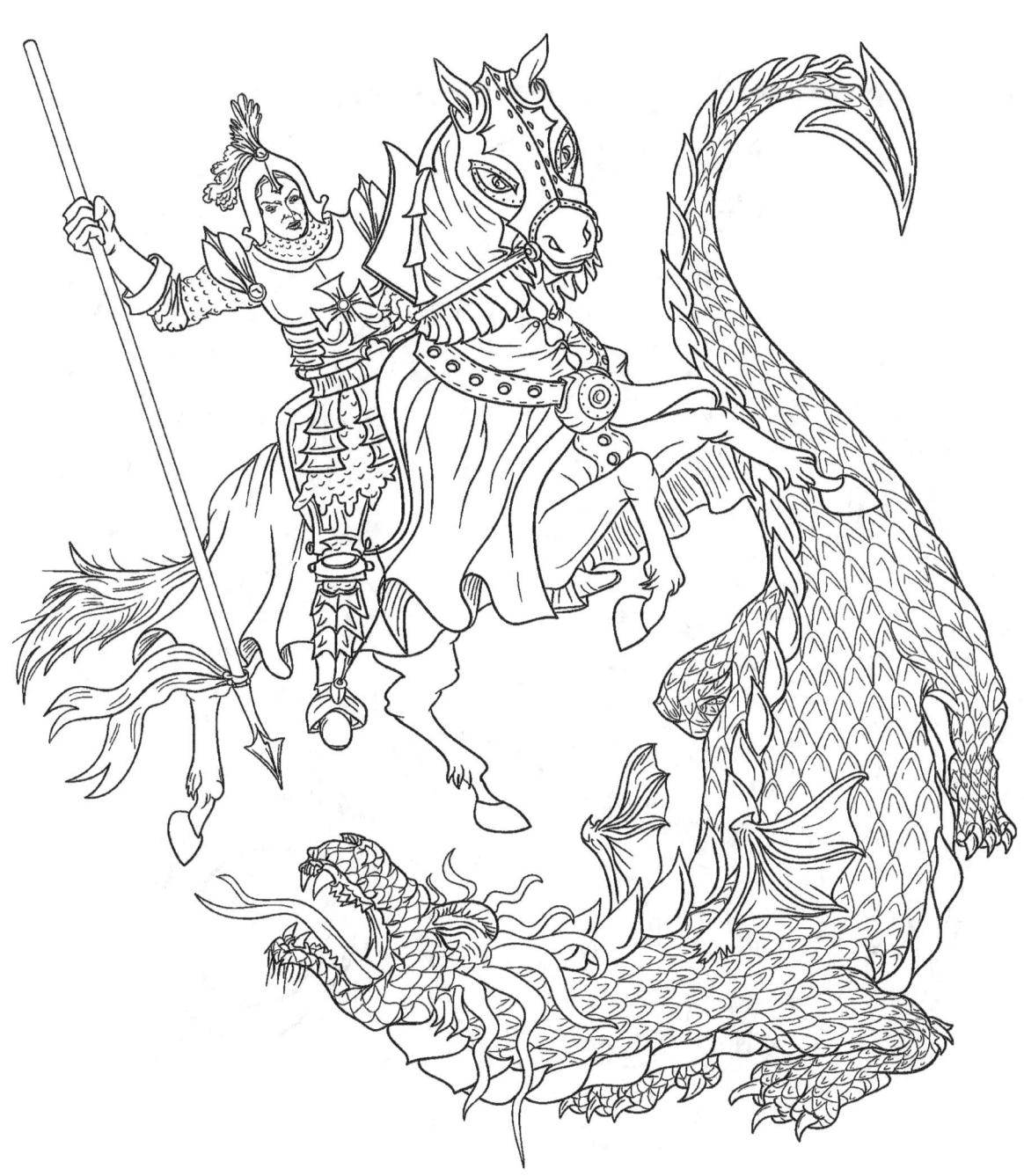

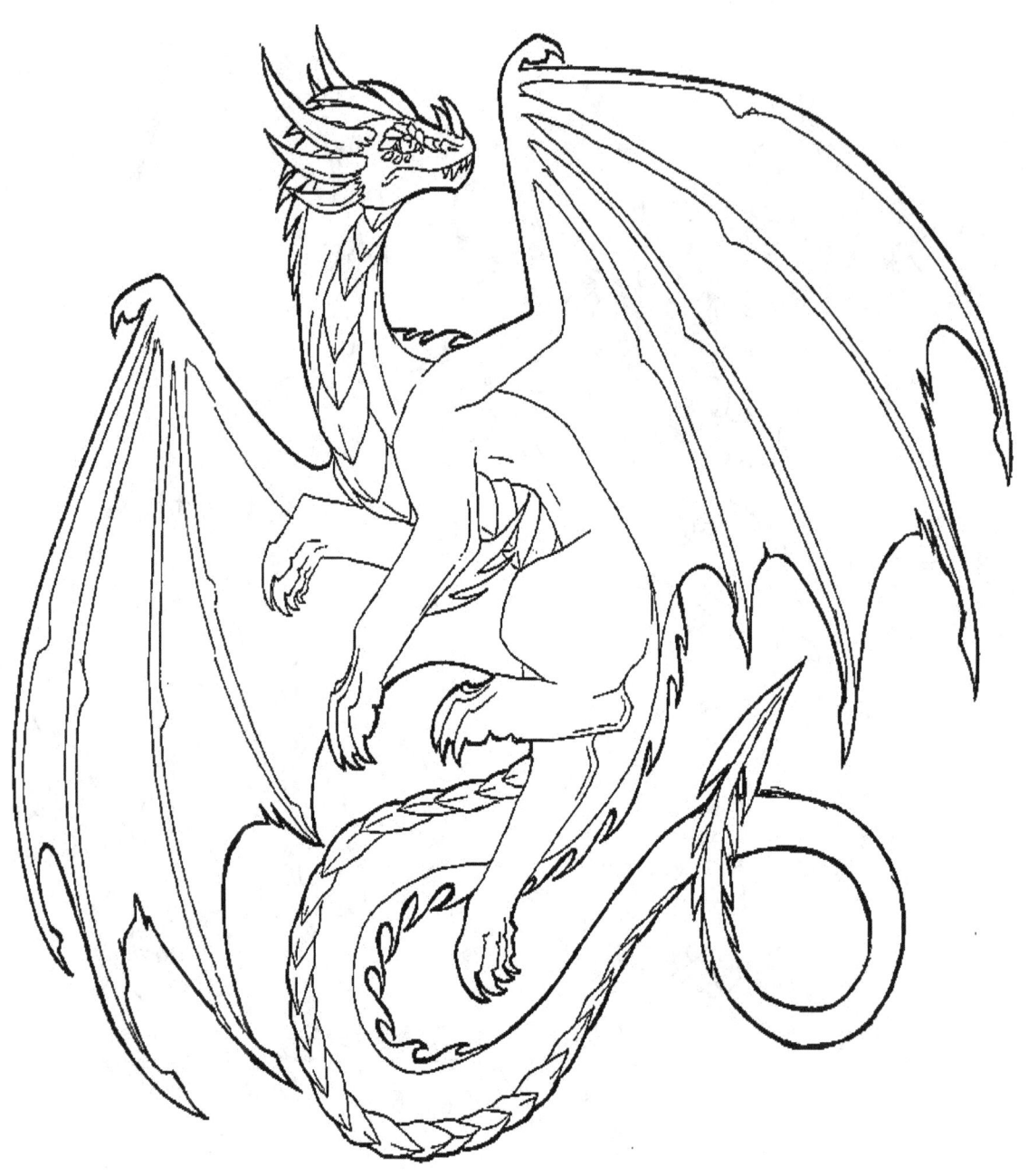

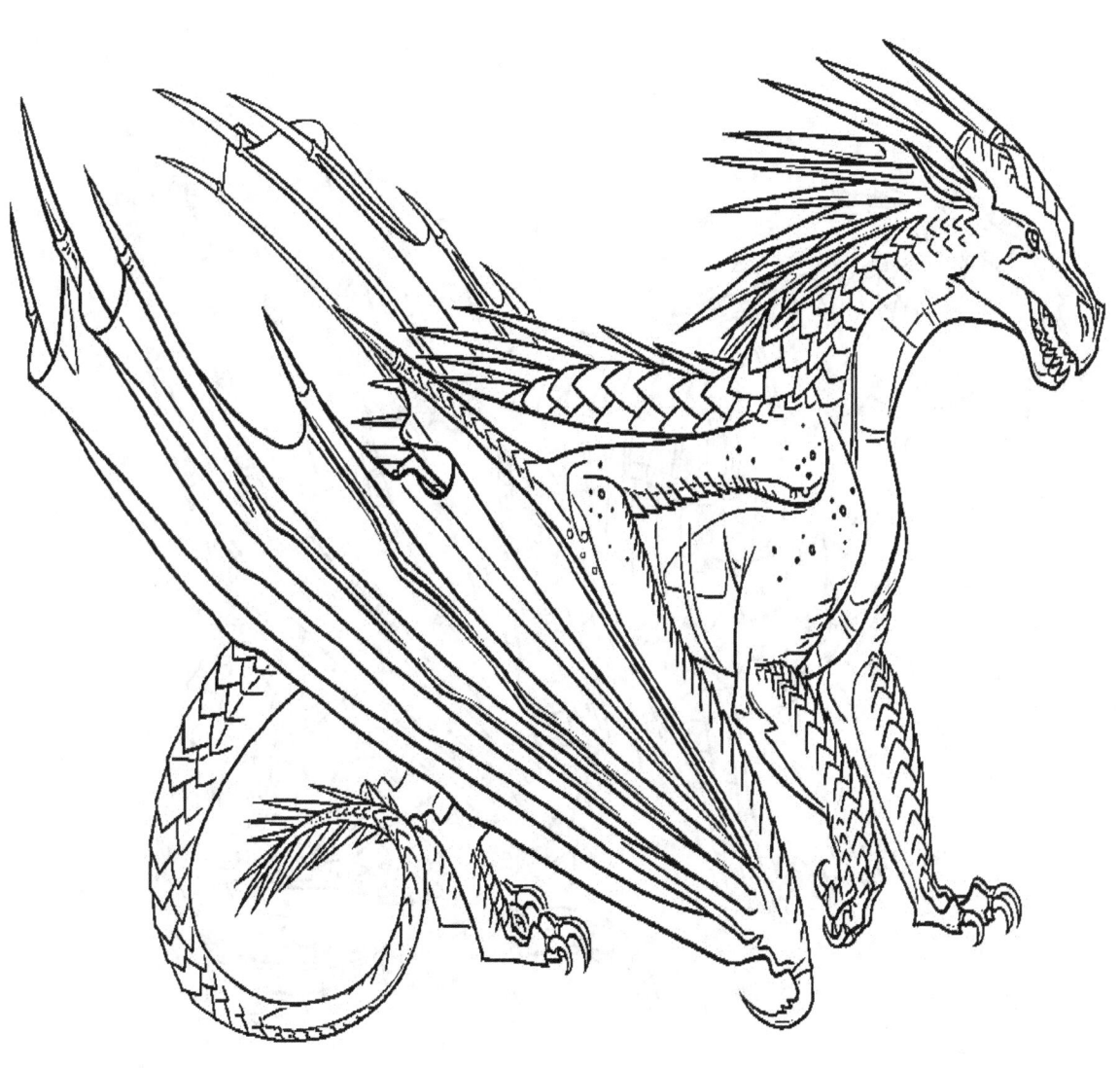

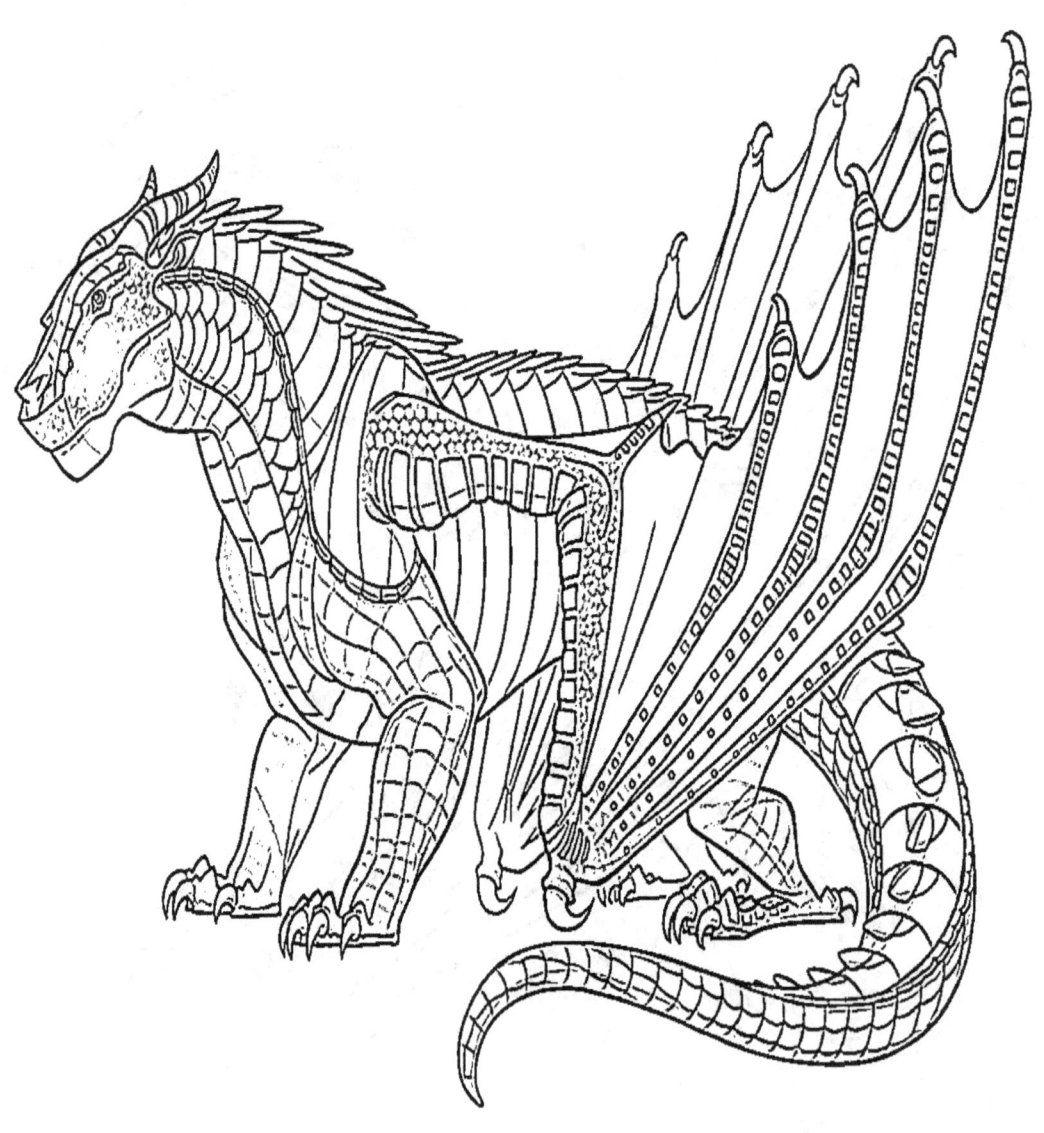

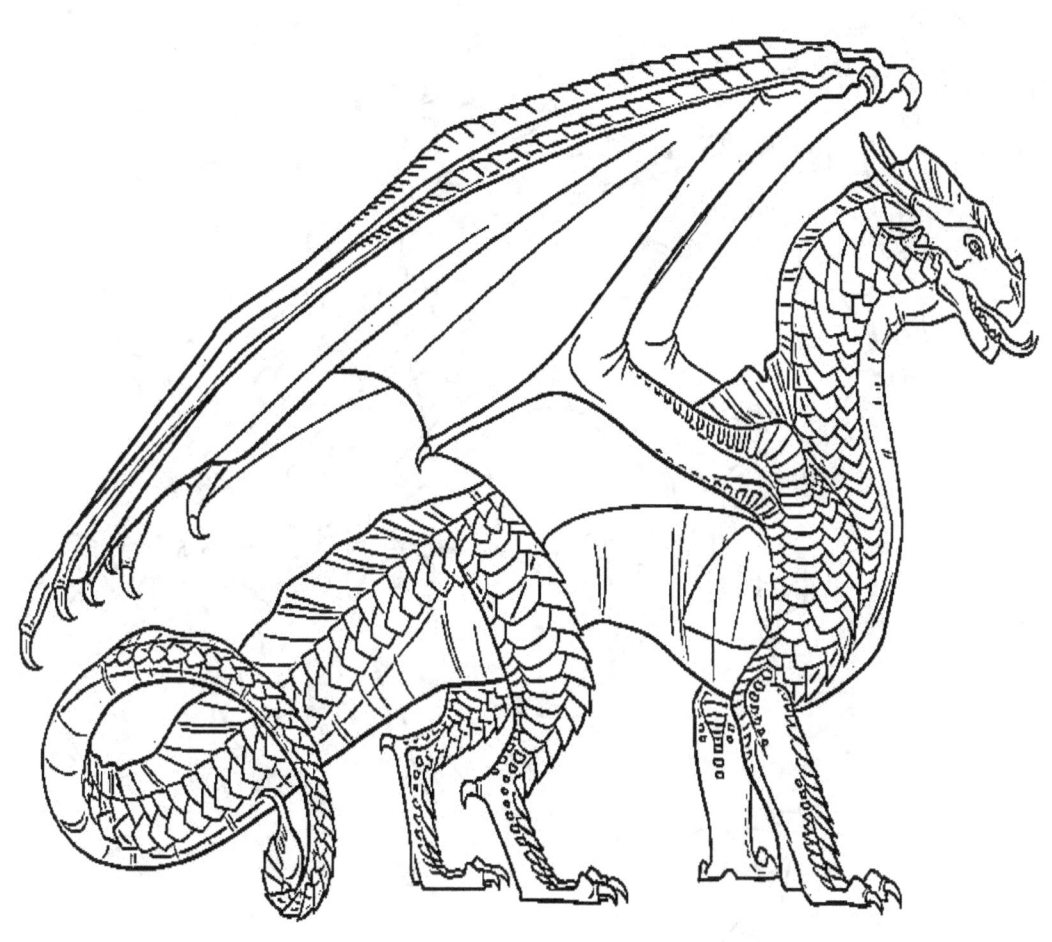

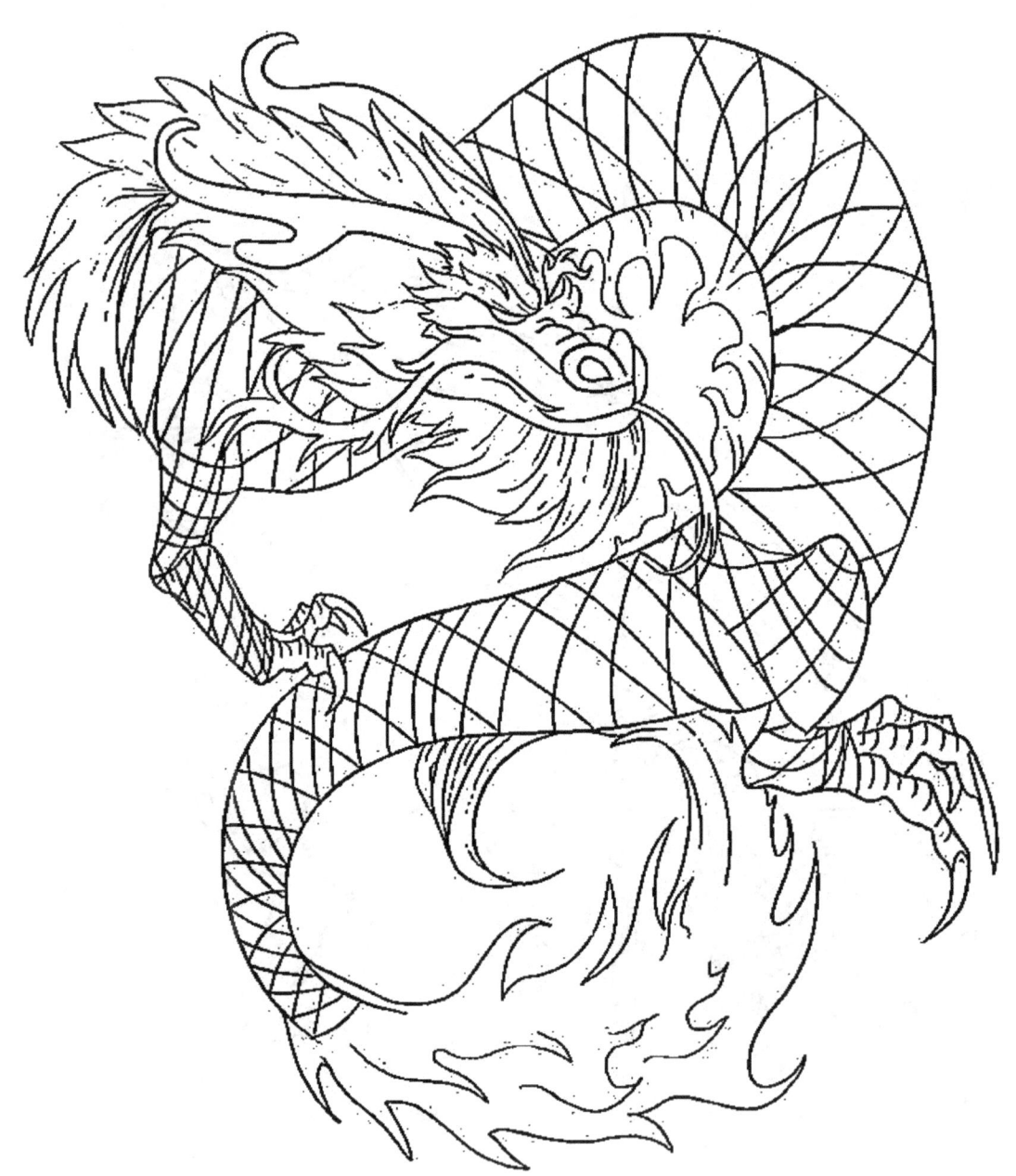

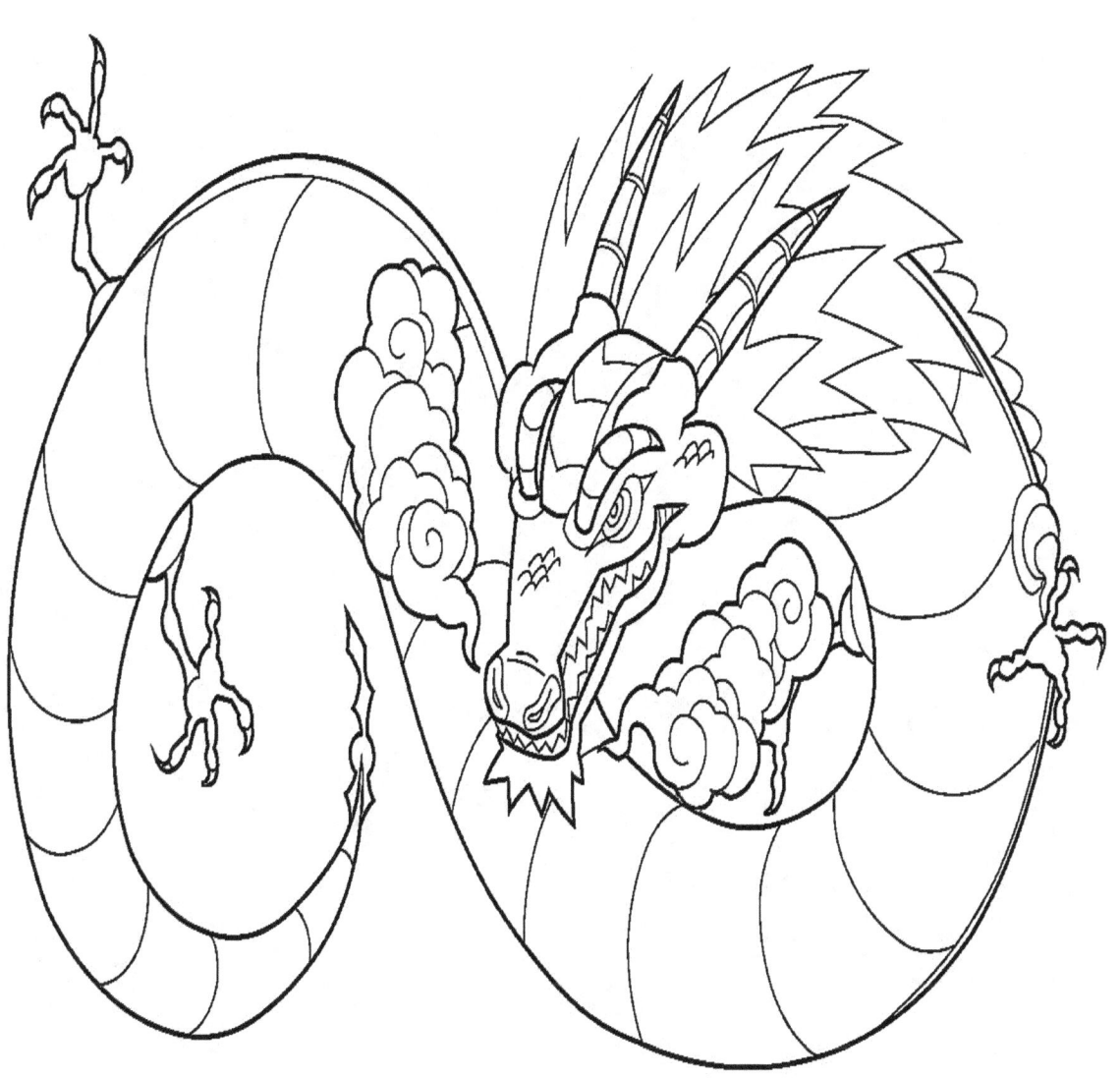